Hustle like Che

HUSTLE LIKE CHE: HOW TO BOSS UP & CHANGE YOUR LIFE

Copyright© Uche Chukwuma, 2020

All rights reserved.

No part of this book may be reproduced by any means, nor transmited, nor translated into a machine language, without the written permisson of the publisher.

Condition of Sale
This book is sold subject to the condition that it shall not, by way of trade or otherwise, be lent, resold, hired out or otherwise circulated in any form of binding or cover other than that in which it is published and without similar condition including this condition being imposed on the subsequent purchaser.

Published by
Eunicorn Productions
Atlanta, GA
www.eunicornproductions.com

Printed and bound in the United States of America

ISBN: **978-0-578-63217-9**

In Loving Memory of
Uchechukwu Nnedinma Ugochi Chukwuma
December 17, 1995 - December 20, 2019

Hus·tle
/ˈhəsəl/

verb

To have the courage, confidence, self belief and self determination to go out there and work it out until you find the opportunities you want in life.

Urban Dictionary

I'm focused on building around my future J.D. degree, not an MRS. degree.

I'm a "girly-girl", I have a high-pitched voice, and I'm naturally a social butterfly- but I'm about my business. When we start talking about working together or are working together, don't hit me with "when am I gonna see you again?" after every interaction. It'll be when you put some work on my desk. If you keep trying to slide in my DM on LinkedIn? Disconnected. Now don't get me wrong, I'm still allowed to be interested in whoever I'm interested in. But if I'm not interested please don't press it, and please don't press me. I'm focused.

It's important to be single and 'alone' for a period as an adult. Find yourself and fix your problems. It's your responsibility and no one else's.

Be happy *Now* not <u>not</u> *"When"*...

Never apologize for having high standards. People who really want to be in your life will rise to meet them.

Ziad K. Abdelnour

There's nothing more **attractive** than someone focused on their **future** as much as you're focused on yours. **Let's both eat.**

Your competition isn't other people. Your competition is the things you don't do. Compete against yourself.

You
are your biggest
competition. If you are not
working as hard as you can,
you will not be as great
as you can be.

> "Walk by faith, not by sight."
> 2 Corinthians 5:7

A couple of weeks ago I was being very hard on myself and felt like I was doing everything wrong. I was more focused on my shortcomings than my strengths. One of my friends told me about the Daniel Fast and I saw it as a spiritual redo button. For the past 21 days I only ate fruits, veggies, brown rice, nuts, natural seasonings, and only drank water (pretty much only things from the earth, similar to a vegan diet but more strict.) I definitely thought I was going to fall on my face without coffee but I was wrong! I even had some 24 hour days where I wanted to keep being productive. I also lost more than half an inch on my waist. If I can sum up my experience in one word: aware. I have never felt closer to God, nor have I ever been more sure of the path I'm on in life.

Leave no room for self-doubt.
The only thing you cannot do,
is the thing you do not do.

There is power in your beliefs. Think positively, manifest positivity.

You are
Braver
than you believe;
you are
Stronger
than you seem;
you are
Smarter
than you think.

A.A. Milne

Joy is a permanent possession:

Enjoy the
Journey,
Enjoy the
Process,
Enjoy the
Growth.

Thank God each and every day for His grace. Pray more Vent less.

Relationships are important do not take them for granted. Do not take people for granted.

It's not what you said,
It's how you said it.

Sometimes I get so wrapped up in being honest that I ignore being empathetic. I say the uncut and raw truth at times, without much consideration for my delivery. While honesty is greatly appreciated, people will always remember how you made them feel. The truth doesn't always have to hurt.

How you speak to someone is much more important than *what* you are trying to tell them. Delivery is everything when practicing good communication skills.

How you treat people
says alot about you.

Respect is mutual, not situational.

I was raised to respect my elders; but I've always been a strong believer in respecting those who respect me. I've had teachers, bosses and family members who have demanded respect out of me, but rarely gave me any. That's not how life works. Authority doesn't grant you respect, respect grants you respect.

Whoever
is trying
to bring
you
down
is
already
below you.

You can't finesse a genuinely good person because it's in their nature to be who they are. You can only finesse yourself out of having access to them.

Don't change your frequency,
change your frequently.

There's this saying that you should match whatever energy you are given. I disagree with that completely. Your energy should always be dependent on who you are as a person, not what you receive from others. If the energy you are getting is a lower frequency than yours, stop interacting with that energy as frequently as you have been. Never decrease your energy to meet someone at theirs.

Those who didn't stick around to help you win, will have to watch you win.

Be **mindful** of people who would rather **gossip about others** than hear you talk about yourself.

Protect your
Energy

There are people who will only appreciate the impact you had in their life when you remove yourself from it. It is what it is.

Don't worry about
what "they" got

Go get yours.

Ask God
to guide your steps. Then,
get up and move your feet!

Is it a risk or an investment?

I don't like to fail and I'm not too fond of things around me failing either: people, relationships, expectations. It's difficult to accept that I can't fix everything that fails. I'm learning that it's important to preserve my positive energy. I'm learning to cater to the things in my life that add to it, and starve the things that don't.

Do not settle for less.
Let go of the things you
cannot change and
move on.

> If you don't make mistakes, you aren't reaching far enough.

David Packard

Are you a *risk taker,* or are you *scared?*

We never *lose*.
We either *win*,
or we *learn*.

It's only a mistake if you don't learn from it.

God
is going to make
all the dots connect.

I can be shaken,
but I can't be broken.

I felt my mood and point of view shifting, I felt somewhat numb- just going with the motions. I realized that there was a lot of alignment occurring in my life, particularly of new beginnings. I'm not 100% sure of what God has in store for me, but I'm walking into this new season with the upmost faith that a part of my purpose will be fulfilled.

You don't drown by falling in the water, you drown by staying there.

Edwin Louis Cole

You can't have a positive life and a negative mind.

Joyce Meyer

You gonna *complain* about it, or *pray* about it?

I don't take "no"
for an answer.
There's gotta be a way.

Any energy spent *worrying,*
is energy that can be spent *working.*

When God doesn't
have your attention
he'll disturb what does.

anonymous

The pressure you put on yourself
can either make you or break you.

There's no doubt that I put a substantial amount of pressure on myself, sometimes to the point that I convince myself that nothing I've done is good enough to get me to where I want to be. I didn't realize how unhealthy this mindset was until I was down playing my own success; I was hating on myself. I am still learning how to celebrate my wins, and strive for more all in the same breath. I'll let you know how it goes...

If you think there are no improvements to make on yourself, you're lying. There's always room for *Growth*.

Honesty
will carry you far.

Which do you want:
The pain of staying where you are or the pain of *growth?*

Judith Hansen Lasater

The butterfly had to be
a caterpillar first.

You owe it to yourself
to be the best version of you.

Are you willing to outwork *yourself?* You are your biggest *competition.* Strive to do more than you did yesterday.

Assume the position you want to claim.

1. Dream about it
2. Make a plan
3. Do it

Losing things doesn't mean you've lost.

When I sit back and think about all the things I have gained, I realize that I had to lose something I once thought was the best I had. I can't keep adding to my life, without subtracting the things of lesser value. I'm getting comfortable with the idea of letting things go, for the greater things to come.

Elevation requires separation. Don't be afraid to let go of what you have, to make space for what's to come.

Whatever misses you, is not for you. Just because it missed you this time, doesn't mean it will miss you the next time.

*Be patient.
Trust the process.*

If you don't get it one way,
get it another!

Your blessings will never miss you; they'll always come back around and get you.

Be Consistent.

Give 100% in everything. Take action toward perfecting your craft: Hustle, experience, persistence.

Check yourself, don't play yourself.

I'm usually on go, but then I hit a hard stop. I spend an entire day (sometimes more) reevaluating how I'm thinking, how I'm moving, how I'm living essentially and then I go back into beast mode. I'll be the first to admit that being on go 24/7 causes you to slack off on certain areas because the lines start to get blurred. I always have to keep myself in check.

I think our early 20's
are meant to be our years of
trial and error. We're bound
to make mistakes, but that's
life's way of putting us on game.

You will make *mistakes.*

They will make you *better.*

Turn a negative situation into a positive one by looking for a lesson. Every pull back can be a catapult forward if you change your perception.

God answers every single prayer. Pay attention.

You will have to relearn every life lesson you didn't learn the first time.

Use the 24 hours
of each day wisely.

Remove any and all distractions on your level up: People, places, attitudes, and habits.

If you want something
you've never had,
you have to do something
you've never done.

Thomas Jefferson

I eat the chips on my shoulder with salsa.

People will think you're entitled because you don't walk around letting everyone know you have been through some tough places in life. They can't imagine you walking around with your chin up despite having been at rock bottom. That's a back handed compliment; trying to condemn you for not letting your short comings define you.

God
is taking you places
where envious people
cannot reach you.

If you are competing with someone you will lose in life; you should be your own competition.

One up yourself.

Today is always apparent in tomorrow:

Preparation leads to *prosperity*

Procrastination leads to *poverty*.

Faith and prayer without pro activity is wasted.

Success Takes Sacrifices.

Distractions
will do you in,
in the truest sense.

-Aubrey "Drake" Graham

Patience is a virtue.

I'm trying to master waiting my turn and being patient, all while applying pressure for the things I want. Timing is everything. I'm realizing that even though I may feel ready for the "next thing" I'll never know until the opportunity presents itself and I jump on it. Until then, I stay ready so I don't have to get ready.

There are things in the universe that God has set aside for you.

Slow & Steady
Do it right, not fast.

Would you rather run backwards or walk forward? *Direction* is much more important than *Speed*.

You will get there when you are meant to get there and not a moment sooner.

$$\frac{\text{Faith}}{\text{Fear}}$$

Don't let fear keep you from receiving more blessings. Your blessings are not only in what you can see now, they are also in what you don't see coming.

When God speaks,
listen.

Always bet on *yourself.*

There is enough time.

People honestly and truly make time for the things they want in life. I know when something needs to be done, I'll find time to do it; whether it's school work or work assignments. If I can't get something done, I make an effort to inform anyone that might be affected by my lack thereof. Don't let anyone including yourself, tell you there's not enough time. You'll find time to do it now or later if you really want to.

Obstacles can't stop you.
Problems can't stop you.
People can't stop you.
Only you can stop you.

Jeffery Gitomer

You are only
responsible for
Yourself.

You want it?
Go get it.

The grass is
greener where you
water it.

Neil Barringham

Make money,
don't let money make you.

Invest in your dreams.
Grind now, shine later.

Don't let anyone ever make you feel like you don't deserve what you want.

Know your worth;
Add tax.

Drip or drown.

If you ever find yourself in an uncomfortable situation, finesse it. Every obstacle you face is a new opportunity to level up. Don't ever let your challenges consume you.

The next time you feel slightly uncomfortable about the pressure in your life, remember:

No Pressure,
No Diamonds.

Eric Thomas

Life is not supposed to be easy; find ways to *enjoy the process.*

The road to success is always under construction.

Anonymous

What's for you will *always* be for you, maybe not now, but *eventually.*

It's not about who did it first;
who did it better?

I realize that it's not important when you get somewhere (i.e. when you move somewhere new, when you start a job, etc.) the most important thing is how you perform when you get there. Are you adding value? No one cares who came to the table before you if you're bringing something that everyone wants.

Men·tor·ship
/ˈmentôrSHip/

The teacher was a student first.

(Mentorship is important)

Who you know
will get you in the door;
What you know
will keep you in the room.

Thank God for all the hungry people in your life; always willing to put more in to get more out. *Everybody eats!*

Help me win; or watch me win. I can promise you that.

Karma isn't about the good or bad things happening to you; it's about the lessons you will learn.

You should never regret anything in life.

If it's good, it's *wonderful*

If it's bad, it's *experience*

Nothing is possible without **God**.

Don't spend too much time focusing
on what brought you to the door.

The next step is to figure out how to get inside. Once you get inside, figure out how to stay there. Once you've solidified your spot in the building, figure out how to build your own.

If you want to *shine* like Diddy, you have to *work* like Puffy first.

While you're working for what you want,

Be Grateful

for what you already have.

Always concentrate on how far you have come rather than how far you have left to go.

Appreciate what you have *while you have it.*

Their perception is not your responsibility.

I get caught up on what people think about me and what they have to say about me to other people. When it's something good, I hold on to it; when it's something bad, I hold on to it even longer. If I could, I would attempt to change every bad opinion people have about me. This is a toxic trait that I promise I will shake. I don't have to prove myself to anyone.

Not everyone will like you, that's not your concern. Focus on adding to the relationships of those who do.

I'm **still** working on it,
but I'm **better** than before.

You will never
be able to control
what people
think of you

You only make a first impression once; people will always remember how you made them feel.

Love *God*
Love *yourself*
Love *others*

Family First.

Treat your enemies kindly.

If they treated you **wrong,** they will **always** come back.

Just because people don't appreciate you, that doesn't mean you aren't

Valuable.

Peep

Understand

Fall back

Do you

It may have broke my *Heart,* but it fixed my *Vision.*

People will continue to do whatever you allow them to.

If you continue to wait on other people you will never reach your full potential of success.

Not all advice is good advice.

Don't let someone tell you things about yourself that aren't true. You know yourself more than they do.

Work while they sleep.

Learn while they party.

Save while they spend.

Live like they dream.

You only live *once*.
You better do *too much*.
You better go *all out*.
You better *be extra*.

Uche,

This is Daddy, Mommy, Obum, and Ekeoma. You will always be remembered as Daddy's Pumpkin and Mommy's Tem-Tem. Uche you said that God created you to be a leader, a discovery, an achiever, a founder, a prayer warrior, a peace-maker, a helper, and that you are going to be the baddest lawyer on the planet. Although you left early, you are still all of the above and your legacy will never die. We thank the Almighty God for His amazing grace and rest in perfect peace, Amen.

Uche is someone who will defend her family and friends no matter what, but also tell them about themselves behind close doors if they were in the wrong. She wanted everyone to be the best version of themselves and if she can help she would. She inspired me to be more of a better person, to make sure I make time for everyone that matters, and do what makes me happy in life. Uche, I'm sorry! I am also proud of the person you have become and I am looking forward to keeping your passions alive.
-Obumneme Chukwuma

Uche was very loving, giving, focused and driven. She wanted to see everyone around her be successful. She was encouraging and inspiring and always had knowledge to share. She was a brand of her own, a powerhouse. Uche has inspired me in so many ways. She has shown me that there is no limit to success. She inspired me as a young lady to be as great as great can be. I have learned to remain focused, remove distractions from your life, and to never regret anything. "If it's good, then wonderful. If it's bad, it's an experience". Uche I miss you. I love you. You inspired more people than you know and surely have left your mark. Thank you for being in my life.
-Ugochinyere Opara

Uche was the kindest soul, a billionaire mogul in the making. She inspired me to to never give up and to always lift others up. The most valuable lesson I've learned from Uche is to stay driven and don't let anyone stop you from achieving your goals. Uche, you're so loved and you inspired so many people. You've made all of our lives that much greater by just knowing you.
-Kemdi Opara Jr.

The epitome of a phenomenal woman. Courageous in every way. A go-getter, hard-working, inspirational. A shepard. She set expectations and exceeded them every time. Uche was someone who saw your potential before you even could. Uche inspired me to continue my journey to becoming a medical doctor. We always pushed each other while studying and tried our best with academics. I will achieve my dream due to her inspiration. The most valuable lesson I have learned from Uche is to keep going and to strive for greatness! I love you Uche and thank you for being an inspiration to every person you met. You were a true leader. I know God is saying "well done."
-Jacqueline Ugwuneri

She would always pick you up when you tripped or fell. Uche wanted everyone to succeed, she was a team player. She was one of the most caring people you'd meet. Her life taught me that nothing in life comes easy and the importance of hard work and dedication. If a goal seems far outreached keep reaching for it until you get there. Don't give up on yourself. Uche, I promise you every goal we spoke about in 2019 for 2020 is going to happen.
 -Jassy

An angel on Earth. The most beautiful girl in the world inside and out. A gnat, because she was so annoying in the most genuine and needed way! She inspired me to follow my dreams. She taught me that forgiveness is key, moving on is necessary and growth is fulfilling. Uche, I love you. Thank you and I'm going to make you proud!
-Dree Taylor

Uche was kind, sweet, beautiful, loving, bubbly, optimistic, a goal getter, a hard worker, inspiring. She's inspired me to reach for the stars and to leave an impact in the world where when I leave people will truly miss me. Uche, we love you girl! See you soon in Heaven.
-Chibuzo Opara

First time meeting Uche, she invited me to her apartment when I was in ATL, even though we had never met in person, she was open to establish that relationship as family. Even with her tight schedule she sort out time to see me even if it was for 15 minutes. She made me comfortable and I could tell by our conversation how driven she was and passionate with the way she talked about law and her future. My first thought was "my cousin is beautiful, smart and she will break boundaries." She was resilient, a go getter, independent and well rounded. She always aspired to be the best and nothing less. I have learned never to settle for less. Uche, your light continues to shine within us and your family and as you watch over us with that lovely smile on your face. Know that you left a mark on so many hearts. Love you cuz.
-Keside Akujobi

Uche was a breath of fresh air. She pushes me to fight past the doubts I have and to be assertive. Uche, thank you for showing me unconditional love.
-Zaria John-Baptiste

Uche you have inspired me in fashion, keeping God first, and being unstoppable. Thank you for bringing so much positivity to every space you've entered.
-Anonymous

Uche was an irreplaceable gift from God in human form. She was a one-of-a-kind, genuine, peaceful, intelligent, comical, optimistic, positive, determined, resilient, loving, caring, supportive, encouraging, deep, beautiful soul. She was passionate about being positive, accomplishing her goals, and letting the ones she loved know exactly how much she loved and cared about them. If you had a goal or dream you could trust and believe Uche would shower you with the support and motivation needed to accomplish it. Uche inspired me to continue leaving a legacy behind and to continue sharing my mind with the world more. It really does mean a lot to people. Her mind was a vibe. I loved the way she thought. Her ideas. And I was always inspired by how perfectly she was able to translate her thoughts to writing so naturally. I still go back frequently to read the story posts on her Instagram highlights for inspiration and comfort. Uche, I love and miss you and because of you, I do things with way more thought and meaning. I'm way more resilient and determined. I've also been making sure to show more support to the people I love like you always did.
-Chinwendu O. Opara

She's smart , fun to be around and has good taste when it comes to fashion. She made me want to work harder. Everything she said she wanted she got done.
-Maahya

Uche was a light of sunshine. She taught me to always put God first and to keep a hustler spirit. I love you Uche!
-Malik Gaines

Che was a remarkable young lady. She was organized, structured, and an ambitious young lady She knew her goals in life and sought after every opportunity. She was for her culture and enlightening her community. Che has taught me to be confident in my decisions and be a "boss" at all times. You don't have to be a seen in order to be heard. Be a leader and the right people will be in your corner. Che was loyal and most of all believed in everyone in her circle. Che inspired me to go above and beyond my goals and never settle for anything below my standards. Che utilized her time wisely and executed her goals. Che made wise decisions that opened doors for herself without the help of others which is why she is "BossChe". She empowered and motivated individuals.

Uche, thank you for being my friend, hairstylist, and being present. Your sense of humor and beautiful smile were amongst your best features. I'm going to miss your banana pudding, dance and fashion shows. Thank your for blessing us with your presence. I love you Chocolate and thank you for making college memorable.

-Breanna Gambrell

Uche was an angel. Uche's work ethic inspires me to go hard. Her encouraging spirit and relentless attitude is just a plus. She taught me that everything I want, the person I want to be is within me.

Uche, there are not enough words in the English dictionary to express my thanksgiving to you.

-Josephine Igwe

Uche was very ambitious, driven, and focused. A valuable lesson that Uche taught me was to always remain focused, persevere, and never be afraid to take huge risks. Uche inspired me to work hard towards my goals and to never lose motivation.
Uche I love you, see you soon.
-Christopher Banfield

Well driven, sweet, dedicated and such a go-getter! Her motivation is like no other. Uche taught me to never give up on your goals, what's destined for you will be for you! Keep working! Uche I love and miss you! Keep dropping those gems from Heaven, they'll never be forgotten.
-Ariatu C. Sillah

A hard working, focused, infectious, God fearing, beautiful, eloquent and rememberable soul! Uche inspired me to appreciate my life and to do the most! To write more, be intentional about my   actions and to go get it!
-Michelle Aba Forewa Quansah

Uche was inviting and inspiring. She inspired me to trust God more and worry less. Health is wealth and that anything is possible. She taught me patience and also to be "extra" because you only have one life to live.
-Khadija Selemela

Uche and I wanted to do similar things with entertainment, and before she left us I saw her actually doing them. She inspired me to keep going and to keep putting myself out there to obtain my dreams. She was ambitious, bubbly, and smart. Uche, your ambition and risk taking is inspiring.
-Caylia Wallace

Uche is someone who is very confident, determined, smart, sassy, and stylish. She's someone who speaks up for herself and others. Very dedicated to school she knew what she wanted in life and she was determined to achieve every goal she put forth. Uche was very family oriented she loved her family so much, she spoke with so much confidence and politeness so if she was putting you in your place you wouldn't even know. She was a beautiful person inside and out. Uche always inspired me, she was so driven she told me she was going to school to be an entertainment lawyer. She was determined and that inspired me so much. Everything me and her ever talked about she achieved or was almost there and I loved that about her. If I could talk to Uche right now I would tell her she is loved by so many and even though she is not here she left behind a legacy. She touched so many ppl and she will be truly missed.
-Aaliyah Smith

Uche is a positive and loving young lady. You can't help but smile while around her, and her welcoming energy is contagious. She remains graceful while keeping it real (being honest and herself) at all times. I am always inspired by intelligent and ambitious beautiful women, and Uche embodies that. Uche, you were always a supportive person and I could tell right from when we were younger. I am sure you are still supporting your loved ones and telling them to stay strong from up there. You are so loved and deeply admired my dear.
-Chinonso Onukwugha

Uche has shown me that there are still great young women in this generation that are willing to take the stairs and not the elevator to success. No microwave success. Well seasoned and slow cooked. She's inspired me to keep grinding at all I want to be in this life and stay true to myself. She used to boost me as a DJ and I don't think she knows it but that made me feel awesome and motivated to keep going harder. Uche, I really miss you. I wish you were able to be here with us on earth and become all your dreams and aspirations, start your career and family, and fulfill all you manifested. But I'm happy you got to move into your mansion up there and are kicking it with all the angels. I ain't gonna ever forget you.
-John J

Uche was a born leader with a bright personality who works very hard. Growing up with Uche, she always inspired me to try harder and push yourself to your limits. She taught me to never give up in what you believe in. Uche, it's been years since we have seen each other but thank you for all the years of friendship from Elizabeth Ave to highschool.
-Jaime Bowman

Uche inspired me to keep going and never give up. She was a hard working, and persevering woman that wanted to go very far in life and she would be the type of person to fill the room with joy all around.
-Ciara Chea

She had a warm, loving spirit about her and wore a smile that was contagious. Her words were genuine and her actions were pure. Uche You have touched the hearts and souls of so many, know that you are loved.
-Teandra Lassiter

Uche's journey to becoming an amazing woman and entertainment lawyer was fueled by faith and the innate need to succeed. Everything she told me she wanted to do in Atlanta while in law school, she did and it was beautiful to see it unfold. Our countless discussions about how we aimed to take over the entertainment industry were always refreshing and encouraging to know that we both knew that we could achieve anything we put our minds to. All of her hard work did not go unnoticed. I am and will always be proud of her. I'm just thankful that I told her that and that she knew I supported her.
-Korede Akinyelure

She was my mentor. I knew her for a little less than a year but she inspired me to go after everything I dreamed of. She inspired me to work so hard and show people my intelligence without having to speak. Everything my name is on proves my ability. Uche taught me remain focused and watch God's purpose align for you. You're absolutely amazing Uche and we didn't get as close but you were an amazing mentor to me. I'll miss you.
-Brianna T. Smith

Uche is one of a kind. She's truly a "go-getta" that is what inspires me. No matter what! No setbacks. Don't take "no" for an answer. She taught me "If you want it, go get it." Uche you're so loved! And still are. Your presence was truly a blessing.
-Mariama Marrah

Uche was a beautiful soul. She inspired me to set goals and achieve them and taught me to always stay fabulous! If I could tell her one thing, it woud be how much I love her smile!
-Stephanie Lassiter

She inspired me to be a bigger and better hustler. The most loving, powerful and inspirational person you will ever come across. Uche taught me to be a boss in ALL aspects of life, period. One thing I would tell her is that she was the hope and the drive that gave people like me hope to be who and what I want to be!
-Jamisha Richardson

Uche was a complete perfectionist. Sassy, smart, funny, caring, hardworking and strong minded. She taught me to get up and actually do what I know I should be doing. And look good doing it. Uche, I wish I could have told you how inspiring you were to me and everyone you graced your presence with.
-Michelle Amelia Macauley

Uche's life taught me to strive for excellence without forgetting to love others on the journey. Also that God is everything. If I could tell her one thing it would be: thank you for being who you are now and who you were on earth.
-Anonymous

I never personally met Uche but I can tell she was very ambitious and bubbly from her Instagram. With my dreams of becoming a physician, the biggest thing I learned from Uche was to play hard but study and work harder. Uche inspired me by motivating me to study. Uche, I wish that we met and became acquainted with one another since our moms are great friends. I will remain motivated because of you in everything that I do.
-Amaka Nwobu

Uche was special. She inspired me to be extra. Be different. Be unique. They'll remember you for it. And it is definitely possible to be in school and live your best life at the same time. I plan on enrolling
back in school very soon. Uche, you were everything a friend needed. Thank you.
-Courtney Wilson

Uche was a boss, extremely hard working. She taught me that your work ethic and will to be great can take you places you've never imagined. She inspired me to go for it no matter what, speak your mind and don't be afraid to just be you. If I could tell her one thing it would be: I've always admired your work ethic and your will to be great! Since high school you always had incredible aspirations and you were on your way to fulfill all of your dreams and more. It was incredible watching your journey over the years. Thank you for inspiring me!
-Julianna Starr Collazo

As someone who didn't have the pleasure to meet her, I'd say she's a gift from God. She was kind, ambitious, and everyone's personal cheerleader. She has inspired me to give myself credit and to be confident. Her confidence in herself and in others is beautiful. It was truly a beautiful sight to see a young woman going after her goals and to share her hiccups of trail and error. Uche, you are a star. The light within you will give life to many souls to pursue their own talents and to make their mark in the world. You are a star because you are and were unlike any other on this earth and your light will continue to shine down onto others.
-Alexis C. White

Uche was lovely and intelligent. A positive role model. She taught me how to be a dedicated friend, to love yourself, and to live life to the fullest. Uche, I am so proud of the young lady that you had become.
-Grace J. Gaines

Uche inspired me to work hard! She was independent. She taught me to never care about what others think of me and to be your own boss. Uche, you will be missed.
-Alexis Lewis

She was radiant, intelligent, a go-getter, inspirational. Her ambition, grace, how full-of-life she was, inspires me to never settle. She taught me that your dreams and goals are never too big. Uche, I really looked up to you— you carried yourself like a queen and I'll never forget it!
-Yauris Hernandez

Uche was headstrong, determined, creative, driven. She was going to do great things. She inspired me to be more driven and outspoken about what I want in life from myself and others. To want more from life. To push myself and achieve more.
-Kendra Lawrence

She was always so determined and driven. That always inspired me to want to be better and to do better. A fun, loving, organized and about her business young lady. I couldn't wait for her to become an entertainment attorney! I myself am trying to become an entertainer. I just always thought it was so cool how we would one day be in the same industry . She taught me to work everyday towards your goals. If you don't, you won't get where you want to go .
-Janay Barkley

"Uche is so gorgeous on the inside and on the outside! She has a sweet little voice but she's such a firecracker. She knows what she wants and puts all of her energy into achieving her goals. She's one of those people who's set on "if I want it, I'll get it". She takes Uche very seriously because she expects others to do the same."

Uche, as your mentor, you made me so proud! Now it's my turn. In the next few weeks while I'm studying for the bar exam, when I take the exam, and in practice, I promise to give it my all, to work hard, and to execute like a boss, because I know that's how you'd do it. I promise to make you proud! You're in my heart every step of the way. This one's for you baby girl! Love always, AD.
-Asendra Davis

She was sweet, kind, and loving. She inspired me to push for my goals. Uche always was very positive and would tell me I could do anything if I tried. Uche, thank you for being such an amazing person when you were here with us. I know you are in a better place now and always check in on your family.
-Martina Michelato

Beautiful, intelligent, kind, outspoken. A Go getter. She taught me to never give up no matter what negativity comes your way and to always go for your dreams. Uche, thank you for always being there and always checking up on me and my daughter. Our memories will always live with me.
-Lexus Archer

She is the definition of a girl boss. She handles her business as needed, while still helping those around her and looking out for her friends. Uche inspired me to go after what I want, even if I can't get there the first time. She inspired me to pursue higher education as well as attain a law degree, and has shown nothing but confidence with the process she went through. She helped me realize that I am my biggest competitor and that no one else has an influence on my life and my actions except for me. She also taught me that it's okay to be me. I may not always fit in with what the crowd is doing but there is always someone there cheering for me to just be me. Uche I just want to say thank you for being you. Thank you again for sharing your passions with me & everyone around you because it has helped me become the female I am now.
-Shanelle Bailey

Uche is a superstar! She makes everything she touches great. Her determination to make change is truly inspiring. Uche I will forever miss you and our talks. You won't be forgotten!
-Dejah Daniels

Uche is one of the smartest people I've ever met. She had more of an impact than she thought, in smaller ways, for instance I always try harder when I think of her. She inspired me to work harder. She taught me to never live quietly, and don't be sorry for being yourself and having your own opinions.
-Jennifer Boardman

Uche was powerful. Beauty and brains. She was educated and beautiful, which was a motivation to all young women. She inspired me to chase my goal no matter how tough it may seem. If I could tell her one thing it would be: You make it look easy and effortless! May you rest in Heaven lady.
-*Sangeetha Santhebennur*

A woman of God. Beautiful. Ambitious. The community was really routing for her and her success. Her work ethnic never went unnoticed. I wasn't close with Uche but her presence was always radiant. She is very loved and will be missed entirely. I want to become a lawyer even more. Especially as a black woman.
-*Adreana Miller*

Uche was very smart and driven. She has inspired me to leave my mark on this world and don't waste time. If I could tell her one thing it would be: Wish you were still here! We have met your purpose.
-*Shetese Roberts*

She was determined and loving. Uche taught me to love myself and inspired me to follow my dreams. I love you Uche and thank you for being a part of my life.
-*Kelly Chow*

Uche was a great person, great mentor, funny, high spirited, filled with life. She inspired me to live life to the fullest.
-*Nishjaiah Brunson*

Private, bossy, nosey, smart, hardworking, intelligent, ambitious, relentless, stubborn, silly, loving, caring, honest, loyal, selfless, adventurous, lively, social, and outgoing. Uche inspired me to work hard at what I want & be relentless until I get it. She taught me to be true to your character even if other people don't necessarily treat you the same. If I could tell her one thing it would be : I love you.
-Jasmine Nwajei

Uche inspired me to be the best me and not to settle especially with career choices. A Beautiful soul, a hustler, and intelligent. She taught me to go after your dreams even when times are at its worst, and always live your best life. If I could tell Uche one thing, it would be: Thank you.
-Anonymous

Uche is immaculate. She taught me to stay focused, positivity is everything, the circle or company you keep will highly influence you, and to reach for the sky. I love you Uche. You're an Angel. Thank you for being a blessing in my life.
-Ayesha

Uche has inpsired me through her hard work and the way she always keeps her head up. She taught me that hard work always pays off. Uche, you are such an amazing woman inside and out, you will be truly missed.
-Jamilex martinez

Uche was elegant. She inspired me through her balance and consistency.
-Wedieu Cole

Someone who isn't afraid to go and get what she wants. A hustler. Intelligent and beautiful spirit. From Uche I have learned to always put my best foot forward in everything I do. I've learned to hustle and to hustle hard. I've learned to work hard and to stop complaining because it'll all be worth it in the end, all the hard work. She's inspired me in many ways. She's inspired me to not care about what others think and the only person I should care about in the end is me because whatever I do affects me. She's inspired me to grow more in my spirituality. She's inspired me to not give up on myself. I want her to know that she has left an impact in my life and so many others and that I miss her dearly. Lastly, I want her to know that she has inspired me to work for what I want and not stop until I get there.
-Lauren Stewart-Massay

Inspiring, motivated, brilliant. Uche was one of many reasons I will not neglect to keep God close in my days going forward. I saw how he worked through her life. She taught me that you've got to do more than believe in your dreams. You have to work hard towards them everyday. Hard work makes the dream work. If I could tell Uche one thing it would be: You inspire me!
-India Saunders

She was so young but such a hard worker who was determined and ambitious. Me and her both were interning to be entertainment lawyers and she really inspired me since we had the same passion. Uche was very beautiful inside and out, great spirit to be around, ambitious, and determined. Uche, we may have only had a couple of moments together but I appreciate every little part so much. I love you girl!
-Paige Magee

I didn't know Uche personally, but from what I can see and from how she has been described, she was one determined individual who also was the most supportive person to her loved ones. She seemed to have a special light that made people gravitate to her. Simply from looking at her Instagram, you can tell she put her all into everything she did. I believe this touched me a lot and given the circumstances, it truly lit a fire in me to do more and do it well.
-*Catherine Owusu*

The literal definition of beauty and brains! She taught me to strive and do better and continue to keep God first. Uche you're a blessing to so many people, people you don't even know.
-*Lamijah Burns*

I would describe Uche as a hard working and dedicated woman. She taught me to strive to achieve the things you want in life, for as long as you have the chance to do so. I was inspired by her intellect, to not waste my potential. Uche I admired you in class. I loved seeing black women prospering in law school. Saddened that your time was cut short. May your soul rest in peace.
-*Anonymous.*

Uche was a boss since day one it's been in her blood. Her whole family is like that. The fact that she was determined to be the best at what she does has touched every one to do better and more. Inspirational, motivational, destined for greatness. Uche, you have touched so many lives.
-*Amina Anifowoshe*

She was the epitome of love and light - constantly embracing others and showing them the way. Her life has taught me the importance of truly using your time here to impact and touch lives in a positive way. It taught me to be an unwavering beacon of light and hope to those around me. Her compassion and selflessness is inspirational. She loved, supported, and helped others in a very beautiful way. Uche, thank you for blessing the earth with your warm, sweet, and gentle presence. I wish we could've had an opportunity to connect and build. Nevertheless, I'll keep your spirit with me as I strive to be a light in the same fashion as you.
-Deonte Bridges

Uche was a beautiful soul. She was determined and knew God had her back. She inspired me in her passion and strive to do better.
-Tamara Santiago

Focused, caring, sweet, free spirited, and angelic.
Uche's life nspired me to put an extra step forward in self awareness. To make sure I can be a vibrant energy around family and friends. Besides staying focused and achieving your goals she taught me to just be NICE. She seemed like a genuinely, caring, willingly, nice person. She seems to have touched every person that knew her in some sort of way.
-Tameika Logan

A young hardworking and determined woman. Uche taught me to live life to the fullest and enjoy the journey. If I could tell her one thing it would be that her light shined brighter and further than she could have ever imagined.
-Christopher Staton

Bold, lively, and fearless. Uche's deep faith, and undeniable confidence was a lively demonstration of what it means for Jesus to live inside of someone.

Her life taught me to do what you love and give each day purpose. If I could tell Uche one thing, it would be that I love her dearly, that she looks beautiful in her anointed white robe, and to say "Hi" to God for me because I know she's sitting right beside him.

-Martha Habtemicael

I myself as a stranger would describe Uche as the most unstoppable, inspirational woman I have ever come across. She inspired me to be a boss, to rise above the rest. She taught me to inspire those amongst you! To be the queen amongst other queens. If I could tell her one thing it would be: Thank you so much. Thank you for inspiring me through other people's eyes. Thank you for showing me what it is to be an inspiration to others, no matter how near or how far.

-Winnie Rono

Uche has impacted me in so many ways ! Motivated me with her quotes , her success and her confident yet humble energy! She inspired me to be fearless. Be brave. Jump. Her life taught me that nothing is too big to accomplish in a world where black women are told they cannot be. Uche, you were the definition of black girl magic !

-Mary K.

She was a beautiful soul who worked harder than most. She's taught me to always put my best foot forward, "while others are sleeping you can be working". Uche, you're amazing, and I love you!

-Me'Saj Closs

Beautiful, smart, full of life, a go getter. Uche loved family and friends. She inspired me to study hard, studying pays off. She taught me to believe in myself and all things are possible. If I could tell her one thing it would be that she's loved, beautiful, and smart. The world will miss her & her future.
-Kym Mayo

I would describe Uche as a purpose driven girl. If she says that she's going to do something or she wants to accomplish something she will do all that is necessary to make sure that she gets just that. She always seemed to have a grip on things and had a phenomenal head on her shoulders. If I could tell her one thing it would be: I'm proud of you!
-Jaelin Harvin

She was younger than me but her spirit gave me encouragement I would gain from an older sister.
She was outgoing and extremely poised. Uche, I love you sis!
-CK Tataw

Uche was an intelligent woman, hardworking, beautiful beyond this earth, a BOSS. She inspired me to manifest. Never give up, always believe in myself, put in the work and trust in the man above.
You are a star Uche, you're an amazing human being inside and out. I am so thankful to have met you and been able to create and maintain a friendship over the years (thank you to Mikayla). I love you so much
-Stephanie Turcios

Uche has inspired me to know and understand self worth, love, to go after dreams and aspirations. She was beautiful inside and out, determined, ambitious, intellectual, stylish, a ray of sunshine, sweet and loving. Her life taught me to set goals and accomplish them one by one. Have positive people around you, take care of yourself: mind, body, and soul. If I could tell her one thing it would be: thank you for always being you, for being such an inspiration to everyone around you, for saying that you're trying to be just as successful as me one day…I remember when you said that to me over the summer at the beach. Watch over us, you are a beautiful lawyer!
-Marissa Savaille

I (informally) met Uche through social media when I started following her. I would comment on her story and she always engaged with the exact word I needed at the time. She was so sweet and such a warm spirit. She taught me to go for your dream relentlessly. Don't let anything get in the way of your God given passion. Uche, you were impactful baby girl! You did what God sent you here to do. Though I didn't know her personally, she was going places. She was a powerhouse and there was nothing that was going to stop that. If I could tell her anything it would be she inspired me to work toward what God put me here to do because no moment is promised.
-Tiyanna Lockhart

Uche was vibrant, melinated, intellectual. She told me in an argument one time that she can live her life however she wants to enjoy it and that'll stick with me forever. She inspires me to work harder and achieve things she would've loved to see. If I could tell her one thing it would be that she will always be loved and remembered.
-Isaiah Miller

Uche inspired me to enjoy the moments and stress less about inconsequential things. She was sweet and open to meeting new people. If I could tell her one thing it would be: your sister loves you a lot!
-Myrlene Sanon

Uche was very inspiring. While following her college journey, she started an organization at Syracuse and I've always been inspired by her mission since then! Uche inspired me to live life fearlessly and with passion and purpose. Create something that will live forever and inspire others. If I couldtell her one thing, I would tell her thank you for inspiring me, and always motivating me to play big.
-Kayla Williams

Uche was positive vibes! She inspired me to stay driven no matter what. To keep going and never give up on your dreams. Uche, thank you for your hard work in school because it makes me not want to give up in furthering my education.
-Sara Nesbitt

Uche was a great person, filled with life. She was a great mentor, funny, and high spirited. She taught me to live life to the fullest!
-Nishjaiah Brunson

Uche was a child of God. She chased her dreams and looked good doing it. Uche you were a light in so many's lives. Your destiny was fulfilled. Rest.
-Chile Onyeyirim

Uche was gorgeous, her presence was one that instantly changed the atmosphere in a room. Extremely kind, caring, God-fearing. Someone that you longed to be friends with. Uche has inspired me in more ways than I can even type. We both shared the same goal, to be an entertainment lawyer and she was two years ahead of me. I would always watch all her instagram stories pertaining to law school and be extremely inspired by how hard she worked and how invested she was in her studies. I communicated with her regularly and she was always very encouraging. She taught me to go for what I want with full force. This girl was literally a mogul in the making. She was so organized and focused, and she really made me realize that if I want to achieve something that I have to work hard, harder than the next person. Uche, I miss you so much. I miss hearing your voice! Please watch over "funky mommy" and your siblings, and daddy, you're forever remembered in everyone's heart.
-*Otesele A. Igberaese*

She was just an all around pure hearted person. I'm a high school student and Uche was my mentor because I plan to go into law. She has inspired me in so many ways in how to navigate being a young black attorney in America. She taught me to always trust in your higher power. If there is a sign, believe in it and trust it.
-*Chloe McCray*

Uche was welcoming. She inspired me in the way she handled issues and she taught me how to fast and put God first in anything I do. If I could tell her one thing it would be: I love you!
-*Uche Orleng*

Uche was a majestic personality who lit up a room. She was also very inspirational, the true definition of a go-getter. She's taught me that there is no excuse to settle for less. Uche has inspired me in my overall drive and work ethic. She was able to accomplish so much at such a young age and had so much more going for herself. If I could tell her one thing it would be: Uche, you're truly missed daily. I still can't believe this happened to you but God gained one of his strongest angels. You've touched so many people in your short life, your impact runs deep through all of our lives. I remember telling you weeks before you passed you continued to inspire me with your work ethic and drive, so happy I was able to tell you that before you left us. Praying for you and your family! Love you!
-Moe

Uche has inspired me to take school and my future more seriously, keep all relationships positive, and that I need to surround myself with people who are where I want to be. She was ambitious, outgoing, hilarious. She taught me that the hard work ALWAYS pays off And FOMO is a real thing!
If I could tell her one thing I would tell her that I love her, I miss her, she hasn't left my thoughts once, and that she's one of the best big sisters a man could ask for. And that I'll keep trying out different ingredients in my smoothies!
-Chima Okwu-Lawrence

She was kind, sweet and inspiring. Uche inspired me to remain hungry as I embark on my life adventures and to always be positive. If I could tell her one thing it would be: We miss you!
-Basil Oguekwe

Uche was so bubbly and funny. She taught me to always go after what you want in life . FORGET EVERYONE and live for you. Stay on top of your goals. Never stop until you achieve them. If I could tell her one thing it would be: I'm not the same person you remembered me to be. I always loved you and I still do. Sisters for life.
-Hawanatu Savage

Uche is beautiful, strong willed and charismatic. From her life I've learned how important it is to go after what I believe in and see the best version of myself always. It's very easy to let life get in the way, beat yourself down and doubt your worth but Uche constantly preached on how valuable we all are and she has inspired me to believe I can do and be all that I want to be if I fight for it and trust God to always be front and center. Uche you are an inspiration - the world needs more of you.
-Sandra Ezidiegwu

Uche was inspirational, encouraging, hard working, and kind. She was a force and so much more. Through our first phone call she helped me find the confidence to step into rooms that used to intimidate me. She inspired me to go after my dreams and bring God and my confidence. Uche, it was an honor knowing you. We miss you!
-Djeneba Traore

The most valuable lesson i learned from Uche is to keep soaring for your dreams and to always strive to be great and be good to others because it'll always show. She was astonishing. She inspired me to love harder. Even if it's from a far. If it's one thing I could tell Uche and the Chukwuma family is that I will always have a place in my heart for her and you all and that I am extremely proud of her.
-Brielle Hamm

Uche inspired me to do me and love myself! She was a fun-loving, sweet and hardworking young woman that didn't let any limitations deter her. She had a life long dream of being an entertainment lawyer and she wanted to achieve that at all costs. From her life I have learned to make opportunities when opportunities look like they don't exist. She would do her research on relationships and connections to make it in places before she even arrived. If I could tell her one thing it would be: I am so proud of the beautiful woman you are becoming. God has truly blessed you and you deserve every bit of it.
-Monique D. Robinson

Uche was kind, forgiving, honest, funny, lovable, hardworking, beautiful. Her drive to be successful inspired me to do better, to want more. She taught me that everything happens for a reason. Always pray. If I could tell her one thing it would be: I love you!
-Dominique Antes

Uche inspired me to go for my passion. She taught me that sometimes you'll have to sacrifice things.
Uche, thank you for being the person you were.
-Brianna Dunn

Uche was a hard working, focused, infectious, God fearing, beautiful, eloquent and rememberable soul! She inspired me to appreciate my life and to do the most! To write more, be intentional about my actions and to go get it! Uche, I wish we were friends when you were alive, I wish we could've had a conversation! You're so bomb!
-Michelle Aba Forewa Quansah

If you never met her you need to. If you did, you'd never forget her. She was the heart of Franklin and had the spirit, joy and dedication to accomplish anything in life. Her name in my phone has always been Perfect Che. When she put her mind to something she made it happen. She taught me to be fearless in the pursuit of my life goals, my life would be completely different if I never had her friendship. Uche, I know I will make you proud, big things are coming soon. I wish you had the chance to continue your success because I knew you were connecting all the dots. I'm so glad you were able to follow your dreams and meet so many people who will be forever blessed by your presence. Forever in my heart.
-Ross Clarke

Uche was beautiful, driven, a force, smart, confident, a star, classy. She's indescribable really, the list goes on. She's Uche. Period. She was an inspiration in so many ways. She was unique. One of a kind. She was so passionate and that in itself was the biggest inspiration. She was a go getter. She put herself out there and made something so special and memorable of herself. The most valuable lesson I've learned from her is to reach your goals 100%. Do not settle. You can do it if you work hard enough for it. Uche, you were so lovely to watch. I loved seeing you strive. It was refreshing and hopeful. But you will never be forgotten because even in death, your presence is STRONG and like no other Uche baby. We miss you. I miss your sweet voice. Stay close.
-Lara Tabet

She was always super driven! She worked so hard in everything she did. I LOVED that about her so much. She was beautiful, charismatic, goofy, intelligent, strong, passionate and focused. She always said YOLO. She really believed in it and did whatever she wanted, I loved that about her. Uche, you've left your mark on the world! Not only me but everyone sees what an amazing woman you were. I'm so proud of you and everything you've accomplished. I love and miss you so much Uche. Truly the best friend I've ever had and everyone around us saw that.
-Zahra Hampstead

As crazy as it sounds I'm a stranger and there's just something about her that makes me feel like I know her. I can feel her energy and personality just from looking through her photos. She was definitely a rare, special human being. I wish I could've met her. I'm sorry for your untimely passing Uche. I really wish our lives crossed paths. No matter how bright your star was shining here on earth, it is shining brighter in Heaven. God bless your soul. Your smile was priceless.
-Efe

She is this ambitious yet lighthearted girl that is 100% real and tells it like it is. She does not hold back, but is always respectful to anyone she encounters. Uche taught me to be decisive when chasing my dreams and to take risks. But to also balance that off with self-care. She has inspired me to reach more people by leaping from my comfort zone. She inspired me to continue putting my faith into God and my career. Uche, you are a truly genuine person that has touched so many hearts. Really one of a kind. Love you!
-Ajaratu Alghali

Uche was a beautiful young lady. She had her head on straight, she was doing her thing, was in college and going to be a lawyer. If I could tell her one thing it would be: You are a beautiful young lady. We are sad to lose you but God knows best.
-Barbara

I didn't even know her but from her pictures and people who commented on her pictures I could tell she had positive, kind and loving energy. She inspired me to follow my dreams, be a good friend, and slay 24/7! I would tell her that she's really loved and she left an impact on the world.
-June Okoth

Uche was beautiful, intelligent, ambitious and fearless. She inspired me to be a go-getter, confident and fearless. She taught me to be self aware and always learning and pushing yourself to be great! Remain connected to God to lead you and give your journey your all. Uche, you were wise beyond your years and blessed so many people in a beautiful way! I love you!
-Jasmine Akujobi

Uche's work ethic has inspired me tremendously!
She was a beautiful, loving, intelligent God fearing woman. Uche taught me that if you work hard enough and trust in God nothing is out of reach! Uche, thank you for sharing your love and being the light that continues to shine!
-Jaeda Wildgoose

Uche was a beautiful soul! Ahead of her time. Very wise, God fearing and a hustler at its best! One thing about her was she was super intelligent, passionate, ambitious and always looked good and was graceful while doing anything. Anything she set her mind to she did it! She has inspired me to follow my passions. To know my purpose here on earth. To be loving to everyone. She inspired me to strengthen my relationship with God and to seize all opportunities of greatness. The most valuable lesson I've learned from Uche is to trust God and his timing. To work hard to achieve your goals and to never give up on your dreams. If I could tell her anything, I would tell her thank you! Thank you for blessing us here on earth. For being an inspiration to us. Reminding us to never give up. For always inspiring us to build stronger relationships with God. We are so grateful and appreciative of your time here with us. Thank you for your impact and loving spirit. We love you and will honor you forever!
-Amber Hunter

Uche inspired me to work hard at everything I put my mind to. Wether it was eating healthy, going to the gym, and finishing school, she was always there when I needed some support. Uche is hard working, bright, witty, charismatic, opinionated, confident, optimistic, daring, God fearing, committed, and beautiful. The most valuable lesson I have learned from Uche is to never stop working hard. If I could tell her one thing it would be: You're truly one of my inspirations, I'd love for us to be closer!
-Christina Abiola

Uche was driven and such a giving person. She wanted success for not only herself, but everyone around her. She inspired me with her hard work and effort that she put into any and everything she was apart of. Uche taught me that working hard and committing to something will achieve any goal. Uche, you have made such a huge impact on so many lives. Your hard work, values, and determination will live on through all of us you've inspired.
-Taylor Dey

Uche was a light. She effortlessly drew everyone to her as she entered a room, and left the people she loved a little brighter. She mirrored the hard work I strive to attain myself. Her life taught me that your dreams are attainable if you have the patience, drive, and faith to achieve them. Uche, you did everything you were sent here to do, babygirl. Your footprint has been made, and your legacy will never fade.
-Mikal Frater

Uche was beautiful, bright, went out of her way to speak to someone she barely knew. Her smile would illuminate from her face and light up a room. I miss her smile. I miss her asking how classes and school overall was going. I miss her telling me to keep going and that it gets better.
-Bethany Keyes

Uche was radiant. She taught me gentleness, kindness and self discipline. She inspired me to love so much more, to be the person I know I am and want to be, and practice gratitude. Uche, I've always admired you and I wish I told you that. Even without being close to you, I felt the light you brought into the world.
-Hannah Ingalls

Uche's life taught me that this existence is temporary so we gotta go crazy every second. We can't think "we have time to do it later". She inspires me to figure things out because if you gotta know it, you gotta figure it out. If I could tell her one thing it would be: thank you for all the lives you've impacted on this plane, continue to do the same on the new planes you'll be experiencing. We know you are needed elsewhere.
-Wole Osuntuyi

Uche is a sweetheart, a special mix of bougie and humble. A determined mindset who is a "go getta". She is stunning without even trying. How she took on her law degree has inspired me to get mine. The most valuable lesson I learned from Uche is no matter what you put your mind to do, do it with your full heart, give it your all. Uche, thank you for instilling something in all of us.
-Lisbeth Almanzar

Uche inspired me to turn everything up a notch and to work harder than I ever have before. She makes me want to be a better person inside and out. Uche was the most beautiful person you'd ever meet. She was so smart and she worked so hard for everything. She was so perfect in this imperfect world. She taught me to out-work everybody else to get what you want and need. Never settle for anything less than what you deserve. I love you and I miss you forever Che.
-Gabrielle Cooper

Uche was inspirational, encouraging, hard working, and kind. She was a force and so much more. Through our first phone call she helped me find the confidence to step into rooms that used to intimidate me. She inspired me to go after my dreams and bring God and my confidence. Uche, it was an honor knowing you. We miss you!
-Djeneba Traore

Uche was beautiful, inviting, and determined. She seemed to live so much life in the time she was here. I feel inspired to do, be and enjoy more. The most valuable lesson I learned from her life is to know your craft and go for what you want. If I could tell her one thing it would be: Thank you for reminding me of what a life well lived can be.
-Kadé Boteh

Uche was my best friend in 3rd grade. She was the only person to come celebrate my birthday with me in 3rd grade. That day she taught me how to blow a bubble with bubblegum. It seems silly but it's something I'll never forget. She didn't give up, which I think was indicative of the person she was even when we were little. She taught me that anything can be accomplished with persistence and determination. Uche's work ethic was and still is an inspiration. I always admired that about her and work to have that drive in my own life. If I could tell her one thing I'd say thank you. While we drifted apart as friends do as you grow up, I'm grateful to have known you and share some memories with you.
-Kristen Paladino

As a person who briefly knew Uche, and thus admired her from far, Uche demonstrated how we all must walk our own paths of career decisions, and that we must not hesitate in situations when we should act. Uche is the embodiment of a beautiful, empowering Black woman. From her commitment to ace courses, her dedication to AJMLS Black Student Association, her personal/professional brand on social media outlets, her career moves taken to make a known presence in the entertainment law industry; Uche's work ethic was proven as a force to be reckoned with. Uche, I admire your grace, beauty, and brains.

-Rochelle Walker

Dear Uche,
I'll probably never be able to find the words to accurately explain the love I have for you and everything you stand for. You have left such a profound impact on not only my life, but on the lives of every soul you crossed paths with. Your smile is so infectious, your laugh so contagious, your voice so comforting, and your spirit is unforgettable. Your light shines now into infinty, and your beauty remains unmatched. I am forever indebted to you for blessing me with your presence, friendship, and sisterhood; and forever grateful to God for allowing his angel to be an everlasting part of my life. I can't imagine my life without you in it and I cherish every memory and every moment spent with you. Thank you for showing the world what it truly means to hustle and excel. Thank you for your selflessness and always being willing and able to lift others higher. Thank you for walking in your purpose and inspiring generations to do the same. You are the epitome of God's love and this earth will never be the same without you here. Until we meet again, never stop showing me that you're still with me! I appreciate every sign and every dream. I love you so much! Congratulations on becoming a published author and continue to rest in perfect peace. Your legacy will never ever die.

Xoxo,
Eunique A. Gaines

About the Author

Uchechukwu Nnedinma Ugochi Chukwuma was born on December 17, 1995 in Plainfield, New Jersey. Uche attended Syracuse University where she earned her Bachelors in psychology with a minor in African American studies and served as the founder of Light On Ebony, an on-campus organization meant to underline the importance of African American students to break through the line of marginalization. Uche wanted each person that came in contact with Light On Ebony to be great, strong, ambitious, successful, and motivated. She went on to further her education at Atlanta's John Marshall Law School where her love for music fueled her dream of becoming an entertainment attorney. From late Summer 2018 to Fall of 2019 Uche started as an intern at Walker & Associates entertainment law firm in Atlanta, GA. Her hard work and devotion soon promoted her to the position of Director of Legal & Hip Hop Affairs. On December 20, 2019 Uche's journey to becoming an attorney was unfortunately cut short when she passed away in a tragic car accident in Woodbridge, NJ. Although Uche's departure came early, her life and achievements will continue to be celebrated and her legacy will live on through her family, friends and loved ones.

For more information about
Uche Chukwuma and the Hustle Like Che
scholarship fund, please visit

www. hustlikeche.com

Image Credits

pp. 11, 33, 57, 83, 93, 98, 123, 132 - Court hammer
LineworkStock/Creativemarket.com

pp. 21, 30, 51, 69, 72, 101, 129 - Scales of Justice
LineworkStock/Creativemarket.com

Cover photography by Devin McAllister

Uche logo by Zaria "Zo" John-Baptiste

Milton Keynes UK
Ingram Content Group UK Ltd.
UKHW020859210224
438192UK00006B/62